I0760182

USING PLANTS FOR STORMWATER MANAGEMENT

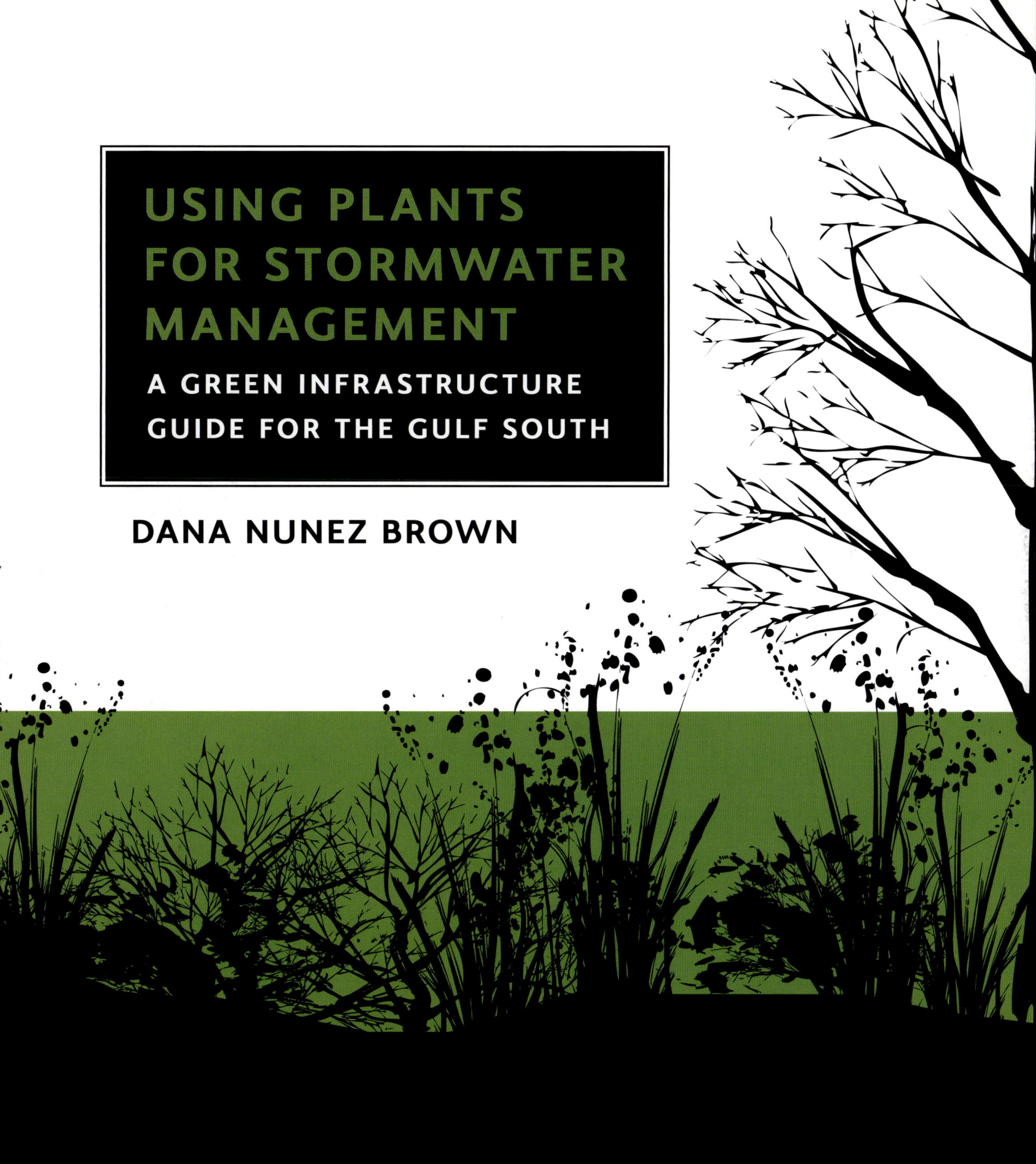

USING PLANTS FOR STORMWATER MANAGEMENT

A GREEN INFRASTRUCTURE GUIDE FOR THE GULF SOUTH

DANA NUNEZ BROWN

LOUISIANA STATE UNIVERSITY PRESS BATON ROUGE

Published with support from the Louisiana Sea Grant College Program, a part of the National Sea Grant College Program maintained by the National Oceanic and Atmospheric Administration of the U.S. Department of Commerce.

Published by Louisiana State University Press

Manufactured in China
First printing

Designer: AMS
Typeface: Cinta
Printer and binder: Everbest Printing Co., through Four Colour Imports, Ltd., Louisville, Kentucky

Library of Congress Control Number: 2013951582
ISBN 978-0-8071-5567-7 (flex) — ISBN 978-0-8071-5568-4 (pdf) — ISBN 978-0-8071-5569-1 — ISBN 978-0-8071-5570-7 (mobi)

The paper in this book meets the guidelines for permanence and durability of the Committee on Production Guidelines for Book Longevity of the Council on Library Resources. ♾

Contents

Acknowledgments

This guide was made possible by the collaborative efforts of Dana Brown & Associates, Inc. and the following individuals:

Dana Nunez Brown, ASLA, AICP, PLA, LEED AP | Photography, Writing, Editing

Amy Norval, ASLA | Photography, Writing, Drawings, Editing

Chris Africh | Guide Layout & Design

Austin Evans, ASLA | Plant Data, Editing

Peter Summerlin, ASLA | Plant Data, Editing

Justin Lemoine, ASLA | Plant Data, Editing

Madeline Ellis, ASLA | Photography, Plant Data, Drawings

Samantha Montoya, PLA | Photography

Robert Herkes | Photography

Introduction

The goal of this guide is to provide to landscape architects, designers, and avid gardeners in the Gulf South detailed information about the use of native plants for stormwater management. The guide is designed to familiarize readers with the native plants most appropriate for stormwater management in specific landscapes. The plants showcased in this guide were selected based upon adaptability to local climates, productiveness of root structures, compatibility with local soils, ease of planting, maintenance, availability in the trade, and ability to take up large quantities of water through their roots.

Stormwater Management in the Gulf South

Knowledge of the hydrologic cycle and how it is affected by a traditional development is critical to understanding how to minimize adverse impacts and create beneficial effects using a sustainable management approach. Under natural conditions, rainfall primarily percolates into the ground and flows as groundwater. It is then held and absorbed by trees and other vegetation, and evaporated into the atmosphere to begin the cycle anew.

Typical structural developments (residential, commercial, civic, recreational, etc.) are planned and constructed based upon the principle of drainage: quickly collecting, conducting, and disposing of stormwater. This engineered approach, which uses gray infrastructures (pipes and concrete), has been the common practice for decades and assumes human intervention in the natural hydrologic cycle will prevent flooding and standing water where it is not desired. Major rainfall events, not to mention hurricanes, have repeatedly proven this approach to be ineffective and unsustainable. We have thus learned, and must be determined to put into practice, the strategy of managing (not controlling) stormwater, making space for water, living with water, and working with hydrologic cycles, which is termed "water management" or "stormwater management."

The typical gray infrastructure approach clears the land of almost all existing vegetation and covers much of the ground with impervious surfaces: roofs, concrete, and asphalt. Channels constructed for drainage are concrete-lined canals usually surrounded by chain-link fencing, and much of the stormwater becomes runoff that does not percolate into the groundwater.

Green infrastructure is the alternative approach that uses existing and introduced natural systems as much as possible in new development. Many existing mature trees are retained. Impervious surfaces are minimized. The banks of water bodies are maintained in their natural state, and constructed drainage ways are designed to mimic natural water bodies and serve as neighborhood recreation corridors. Green infrastructure is an important strategy in environmentally sensitive land development and one that can lower overall development costs.

Most development has followed gray infrastructure practices, and now we must work to retrofit existing built environments, as well as design new environments that utilize the natural processes embodied in green infrastructure. Stormwater management techniques imitate these natural processes to filter, clean, and slow stormwater in the built world to near the same levels that occur in a natural ecosystem. This approach is also known as Low Impact Development (LID). The native plants that are used in these environments, and which are useful in the built ecologies, are the focus of this book.

Plants' Role in Stormwater Management

Stormwater management systems are designed to manage each drop of rainwater where it falls. Plants can be used in a series of small elements known as stormwater best management practices (BMPs). BMPs can take many different forms, but all have at least one of the following functions: infiltration, filtration, and/or detention/retention.

Infiltration BMPs such as bioretention cells or rain gardens catch water and allow it to infiltrate into the ground. At the same time, the plants clean and absorb the water percolating through the soil.

Filtration BMPs use native plants to filter stormwater runoff as it moves from one area to another. Bioswales are common filtration BMPs that filter pollutants out of rainwater by absorbing water and contaminants through the following processes: dissolving pollutants through biochemical processes in their roots, catching pollutants by allowing them to cling to their roots, and holding the water around their roots and allowing bugs to render the pollutants harmless through metabolic processes.

Detention or retention BMPs are large depressions in the topography of a site, providing space to hold and temporarily store rainwater. This gives the downstream system time to drain before the upstream water reaches that area, thus reducing downstream flooding. Retention ponds or basins, also known as wet ponds, are designed to permanently hold water as an amenity and provide freeboard space for temporary stormwater storage. Detention ponds or basins, also known as dry ponds, fully drain and remain dry when not being replenished by rainfall or runoff. Stormwater wetlands are detention BMPs that remove pollutants and sediments by filtering flows through native vegetation and then settling due to slow shallow depths. Detention and retention ponds as well as stormwater wetlands can be used to remove pollutants through settling and absorption by plants. Plants uptake pollutants and sequester them in stems and leaves, and break them down through biochemical processes.

Using native plants for stormwater management has many benefits. Maintenance costs are less than alternative methods because the use of natural plant processes requires less equipment and labor since plants do most of the work. Also, once native plants are established, they require less fertilizer, pesticides, and watering than exotic species. Integrated pest and disease management is recommended as part of a sustainable stormwater management system, which utilizes bugs and other natural predators to control pests and diseases that can harm the native plants. In this way, pesticides and herbicides are usually unnecessary. Proper design of the plants' growing media and use of mulch makes the fertilizers also unnecessary. The use of native plants restores biodiversity and the natural heritage lost through human development.

Plant Communities in Southern and Coastal Louisiana

This guide explores the habitats of Southern Louisiana and the freshwater plant communities that exist within each habitat to give a better understanding of their natural growing conditions. The user is encouraged to mimic the natural forming of native habitats to create environmentally sensitive landscapes that manage stormwater. Below is a map of the wildlife habitats of Southern Louisiana showcased in this guide, excluding the Pine Forest habitat.

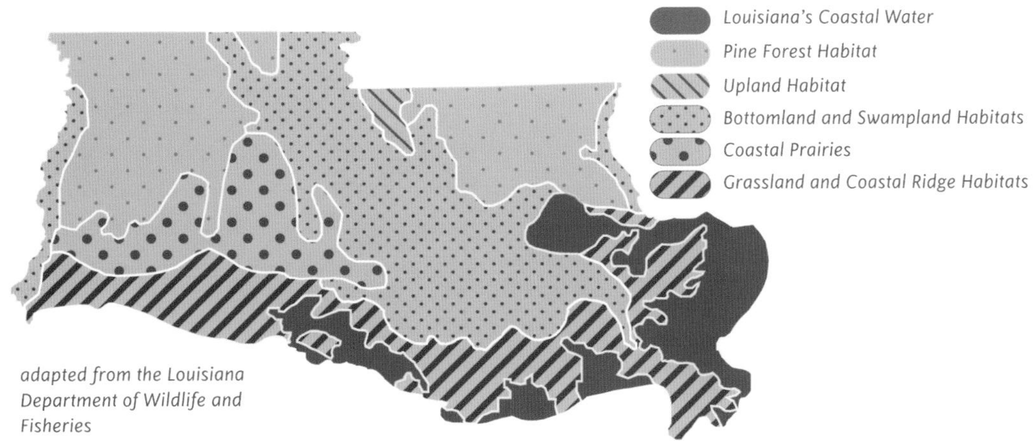

adapted from the Louisiana Department of Wildlife and Fisheries

Plant Communities in Southern and Coastal Louisiana

Upland Habitat **[1a 1b 1c]**

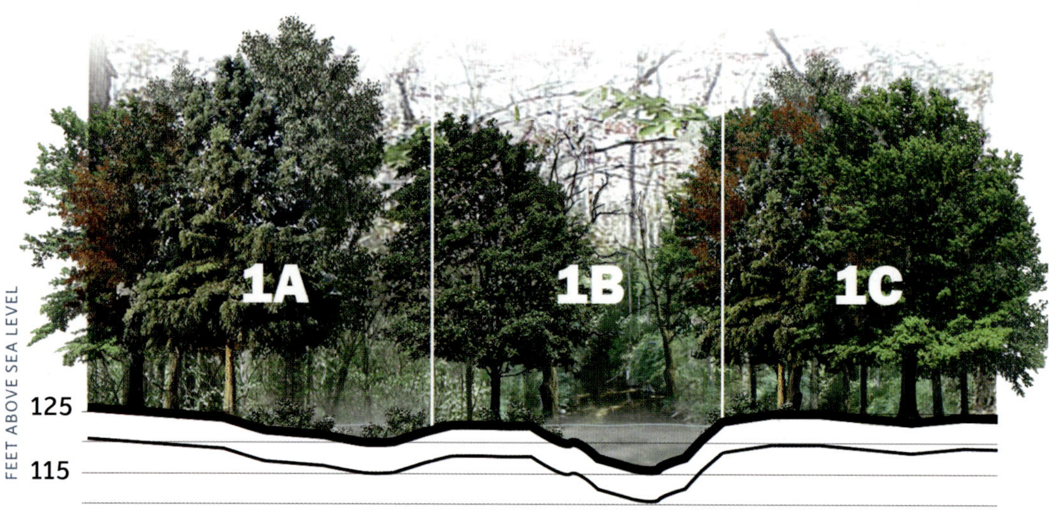

Bottomland Habitat **[2a 2b 2c]**

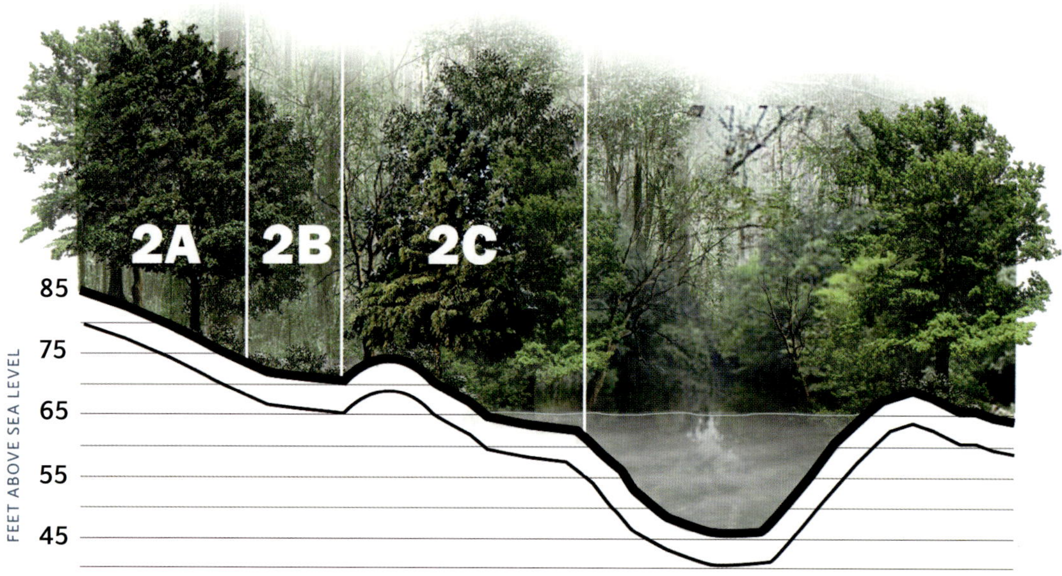

Upland habitats occur along the upper terraces of the Gulf South and are not dependent upon major river systems. The plant communities within the Upland habitat include Flatwoods Ponds, Small Stream Forests, and Hardwood Flatwoods Forests.

1A. Flatwoods Ponds: Small, natural depressions that create wetlands and range from less than one acre to thirty or forty acres

1B. Small Stream Forests: Occur along small streams, these narrow wetlands flood seasonally

1C. Harwood Flatwoods Forests: Occur on poorly drained soils, allowing water to pool during the wet season

adapted from Louisiana Department of Wildlife and Fisheries

Bottomland habitats line major river systems and are dependent upon the alternating wet and dry periods brought on by seasonal flooding to maintain their ecological balance. Bottomland Hardwood Forests, Scrub/Shrub Swamps, and Batture are plant communities found within the Bottomland habitat.

2A. Bottomland Hardwood Forests: provide water quality maintenance, habitat for a variety of fish and wildlife species, flooding regulation and stream recharge

2B. Scrub/Shrub Swamps: Low, flat, freshwater swamps with large shrubs and small trees less than thirty-five feet in height; this community follows disturbances such as cutting or natural blowdown of canopy trees

2C. Batture lands: Develop on the slope between natural levees and major rivers and streams; first plant community (pioneer community) to develop on newly formed sand bars and river margins

adapted from Louisiana Department of Wildlife and Fisheries

Plant Communities in Southern and Coastal Louisiana

Swampland Habitat **[3a 3b]**

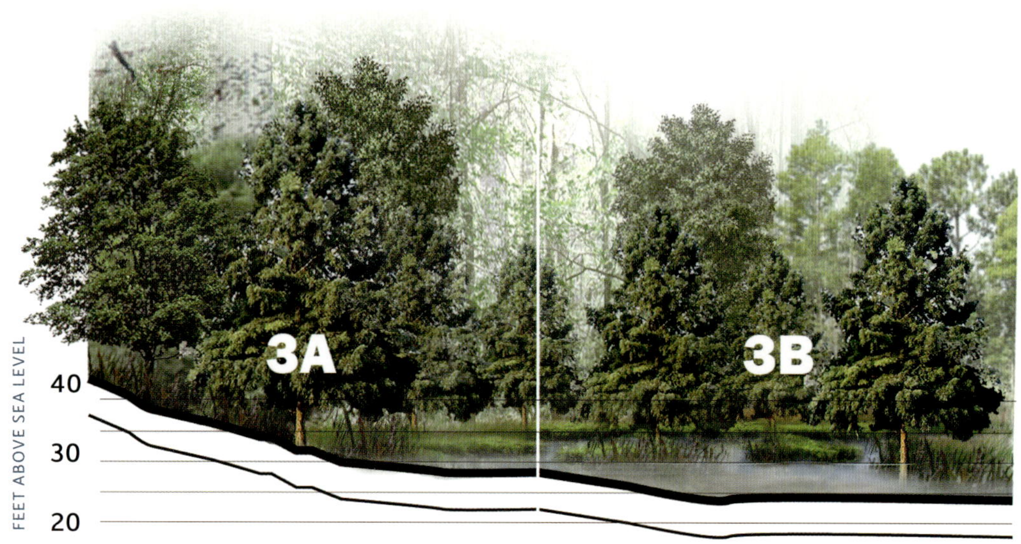

Grassland Habitat **[4a 4b]**

Swampland habitats grow in alluvial floodplains either along rivers and streams or in natural depressions and swales. Swamps experience almost continuous flooding, making plant species tolerant of extended periods of partial inundation. The difference between Backswamps and Deepwater Swamps is the major division in Swampland habitats.

3A. Backswamps: Pond Cypress and Black Gum are the prevalent plant species where the water is detached from the active stream channels, remaining relatively still in natural depressions

3B. Deepwater Swamps: Cypress and Tupelo stands dominate the overstory population; the stands are usually the same age because sapling establishment conditions happen very infrequently

adapted from Louisiana Department of Wildlife and Fisheries

Grassland consists primarily of low herbaceous plant cover with stands of trees occurring along the better-drained, outer edges. Coastal Prairies and Freshwater Marshes are two plant communities among the freshwater habitat.

4A. Coastal Prairies: May be divided into two main types, upland dry and marsh-fringing prairie; both types occur on poorly drained clay soils that create a pan six to eighteen inches below the surface and rely on occasional burning to prevent overstory domination

4B. Freshwater Marshes: Occur on the northern-most edge of the coast adjacent to brackish marshes or along coastal freshwater bays with small pools peppered throughout; have the greatest plant diversity among all marsh types and are important habitats for a variety of young marine species and migratory waterfowl

adapted from Louisiana Department of Wildlife and Fisheries

Plant Communities in Southern and Coastal Louisiana

Coastal Ridges Habitat **[5a 5b 5c]**

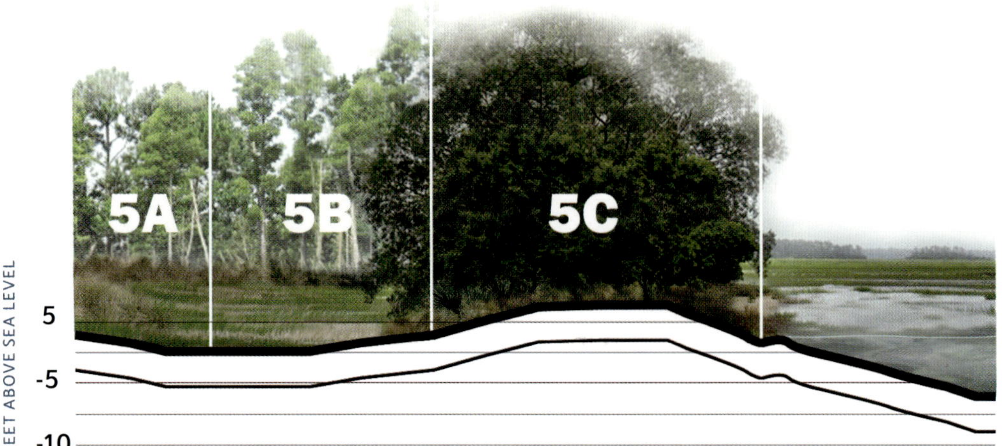

Coastal Ridges occur along the coast creating a natural line of defense against hurricane storm surges. Live Oak Coastal Forests (Cheniers) and associated Coastal Dune Grasslands and Shrub Thickets form the plant communities within the Coastal Ridge habitat.

5A. Coastal Dune Shrub Thickets: Typically dry landscapes containing shrub thickets that can tolerate a level of salt spray

5B. Coastal Dune Grasslands: Occur along elevated backshores or ridges but are becoming increasingly rare due to washout from storm surges and floods

5C. Live Oak Coastal Forest: Develop on natural ridges formed from deltaic and tidal sedimentation; plant species composition varies along the coast with the most diversity occurring in southeastern Louisiana in the Live Oak Natural Levee Forests

adapted from Louisiana Department of Wildlife and Fisheries

How to Use this Guide

- Use plant community information as a visual model for native growing conditions
- Use icons depicting sun exposure, water requirements, and physical characteristics for plant selection specific to user's site conditions
- Use pictures, drawings, and descriptions to identify native plants used for stormwater management

Deciduous Trees

for Stormwater Management

Deciduous Trees Master List

for Stormwater Management

Acer negundo

Boxelder

sun soils characteristics

Average dimensions
50' x 35'

- Bright green foliage
- Irregular shape
- Fast grower, weak-wooded

plant communities

[1a 1b 1c] **[2a** 2b 2c**]** [3a 3b] [4a 4b] **[**5a 5b **5c]**

Acer rubrum

Red Maple

Average dimensions

60' x 40'

sun

soils

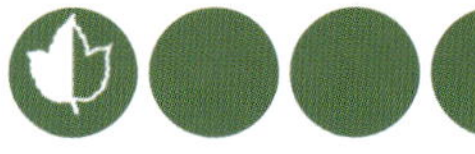

characteristics

- Fast grower
- Small shade tree
- Irregular shape
- Great seed color in spring
- Beautiful fall color
- Great pollinator
- Some cultivars are more wind resistant than others

plant communities

[1a 1b 1c] [2a 2b 2c] [3a 3b] [4a 4b] [5a 5b 5c]

Aralia spinosa

Devil's Walking Stick

Average dimensions
35' x 10'

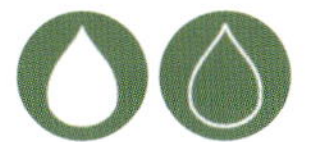

sun soils characteristics

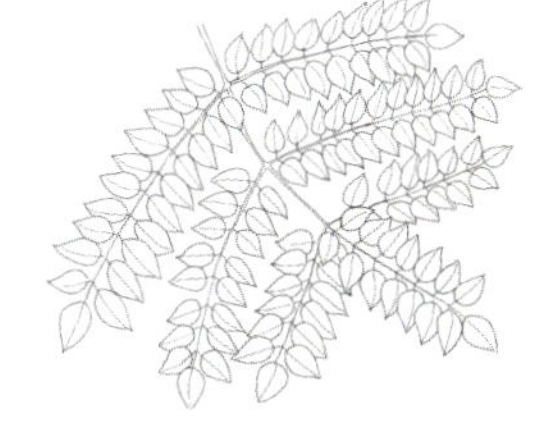

- Sharp spines
- Be careful planting in areas where people are active
- Loose, open form
- Understory to mid-canopy tree along streams
- Colonizer but not considered invasive

plant communities

[1a 1b **1c**] [2a 2b 2c] [3a 3b] [4a 4b] [5a 5b 5c]

Betula nigra

River Birch

Average dimensions
50' x 35'

sun

soils

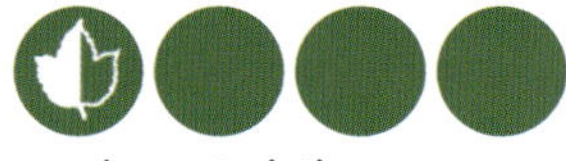

characteristics

- Fast grower
- Great for slope stabilization near streams
- Open form
- Beautiful bark and drooping branches
- Performs well in urban areas
- Horizontally aggressive surface root system can be damaging to pavement and small building foundations, etc., but will not damage pipes because roots will not go deep enough

plant communities

[1a **1b** 1c] [2a 2b **2c**] [3a 3b] [4a 4b] [5a 5b 5c]

Carpinus caroliniana

Ironwood

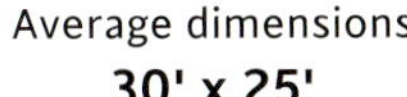

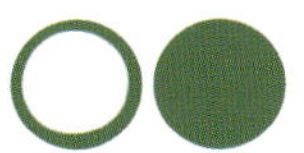

- Known as 'Musclewood' for the forms that the trunk takes on
- Non-showy tree
- Good filler tree
- Provides fruits and seeds
- Good nesting for birds

plant communities

[1a **1b** 1c] [2a 2b 2c] [3a 3b] [4a 4b] [5a 5b 5c]

Carya aquatica

Bitter Pecan

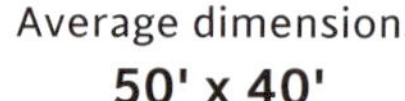

sun soils characteristics

- High canopy
- Bright green leaves
- Open form
- Messy, as it drops small branches, pecans, and pecan shells half the year

plant communities

[1a 1b 1c] [2a 2b 2c] [3a 3b] [4a 4b] [5a 5b 5c]

Catalpa bignonioides

Southern Catalpa

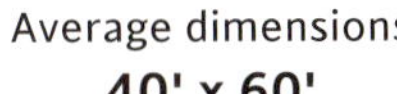

sun soils characteristics

- Large leaves
- Beautiful flowers in spring
- Large seed pods
- Messy when shedding
- Large tree with relatively compact branching

plant communities

[1a 1b 1c] [2a 2b 2c] [3a 3b] [4a 4b] [5a 5b 5c]

Celtis laevigata

Hackberry

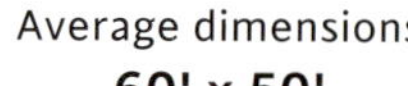

Average dimensions
60' x 50'

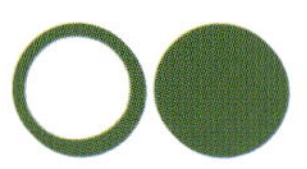

sun

soils

characteristics

- Bright green leaves
- Dense canopy
- Interesting, corky bark
- Messy tree
- Berries attract birds
- Not recommended near paths or parking areas
- Provides fruits and seeds
- Good nesting for birds
- Extremely adaptive; can grow virtually anywhere, though aesthetics can suffer

plant communities

[1a 1b **1c**] [**2a** 2b **2c**] [3a 3b] [4a 4b] [5a 5b **5c**]

Chionanthus virginicus

White Fringe Tree

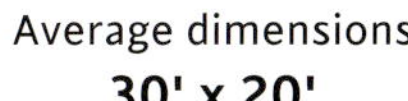

sun soils characteristics

- Very showy, white, and strong-smelling flowers in spring
- Can be used as understory species or in full sun
- Drought tolerant despite its preference for moist soils
- Excellent substitute for Flowering Dogwood in Deep South

plant communities

[1a 1b 1c] [2a 2b 2c] [3a 3b] [4a 4b] [5a 5b 5c]

Cornus drummondii

Rough-Leaf Dogwood

Average dimensions
30' x 20'

sun

soils

characteristics

- Provides fruits and seeds
- Good nesting for birds
- Understory tree
- Occurs along woodland edges

plant communities

[1a 1b 1c] [2a 2b 2c] [3a 3b] [4a 4b] [5a 5b 5c]

Crataegus opaca

Mayhaw

Average dimensions
20' x 20'

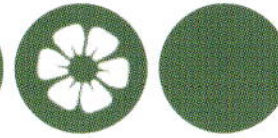

sun soils characteristics

- Flowers in early spring
- Showy red fruit in summer
- Fruit used to make jellies
- Tolerates moist soil

plant communities
[1a 1b 1c] [2a 2b 2c] [3a 3b] [4a 4b] [5a 5b 5c]

Cyrilla racemiflora

Leatherwood, Titi

sun soils characteristics

Average dimensions
30' x 15'

- Great pollinator
- Grows in dense thickets or as singular specimen
- Fragrant white flowers in late spring

plant communities

[1a 1b 1c] [2a 2b 2c] [3a 3b] [4a 4b] [5a 5b 5c]

Diospyros virginiana

Common Persimmon

Average dimensions
50' x 25'

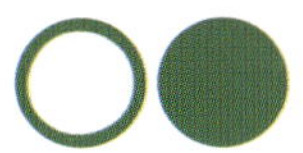

sun soils characteristics

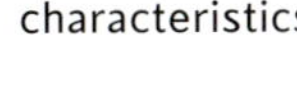

- Open, irregular form
- Glossy leaves
- Edible fruit but bitter when not ripe
- Messy in the fall
- Not recommended where branches would hang over pavement
- Recognizable scale-like bark
- Seed can be roasted as a coffee substitute

plant communities

[1a 1b 1c] [2a 2b 2c] [3a 3b] [4a 4b] [5a 5b **5c**]

Fagus grandifolia

American Beech

sun soils characteristics

Average dimensions
100' x 70'

- Large canopy with dense branching
- Holds fall foliage through winter
- Good shade tree
- Majestic form; great specimen tree
- Difficult to grow

plant communities

[1a **1b** 1c] [2a 2b 2c] [3a 3b] [4a 4b] [5a 5b 5c]

Fraxinus pennsylvanica

Green Ash

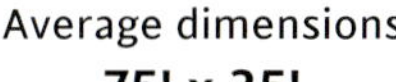

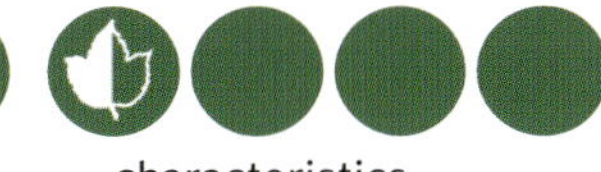

sun soils characteristics

- Irregular, open branching form
- Fast grower
- Weak-wooded
- Not recommended near structures
- Messy seeds

plant communities

[1a 1b 1c] [2a 2b 2c] [3a 3b] [4a 4b] [5a 5b 5c]

Halesia diptera

Silver-Bell

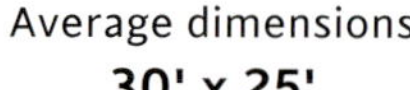

Average dimensions
30' x 25'

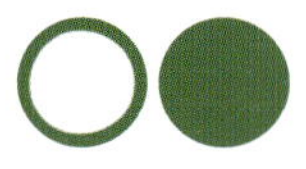

sun soils characteristics

- Small white flowers bloom in spring
- Semi-dense canopy
- Medium-sized tree
- Yellow fall color

plant communities

[1a **1b** 1c] [2a 2b 2c] [3a 3b] [4a 4b] [5a 5b 5c]

Ilex decidua

Possumhaw

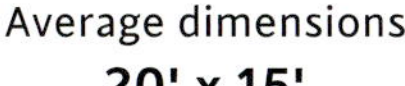

Average dimensions
20' x 15'

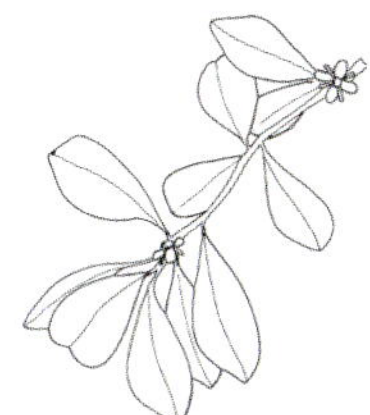

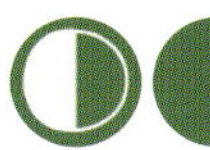
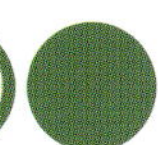

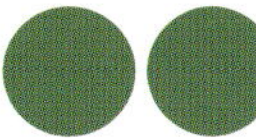
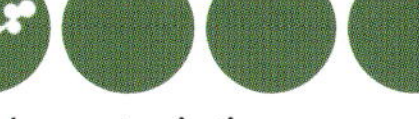

sun soils characteristics

- Small deciduous tree
- Slow growing
- Yellow fall color
- Attractive red fruit when mature but mildly toxic
- Desires and thrives in moist soil

plant communities

[1a 1b 1c] [**2a** 2b 2c] [3a 3b] [4a 4b] [5a 5b 5c]

Magnolia ashei

Ashe Magnolia

Average dimensions
30' x 15'

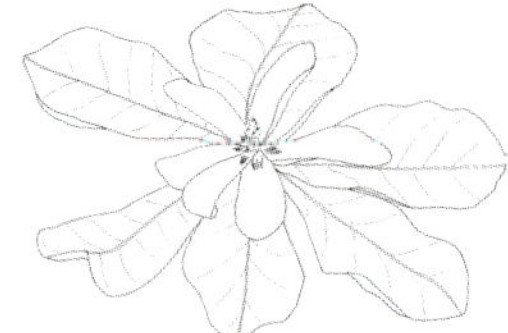

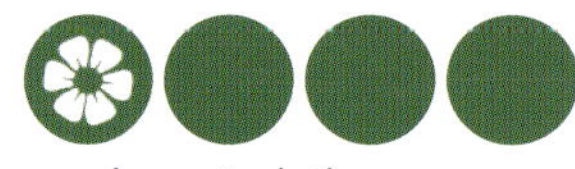

sun soils characteristics

- Blooms in early summer
- Fragrant blossoms
- White saucer-shaped flower

plant communities
[1a **1b 1c**] [2a 2b 2c] [3a 3b] [4a 4b] [5a 5b 5c]

Nyssa aquatica

Water Tupelo

Average dimensions
80' x 40'

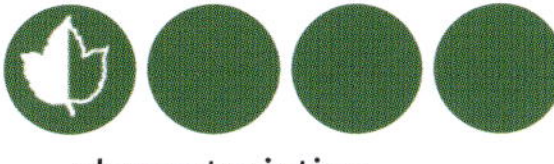

sun soils characteristics

- Long-lived swamp tree
- Mature trees produce timber
- Rarely seen in the trade

plant communities

[1a 1b 1c] [2a 2b 2c] [3a **3b**] [4a 4b] [5a 5b 5c]

Nyssa sylvatica

Black Gum

Average dimensions
80' x 40'

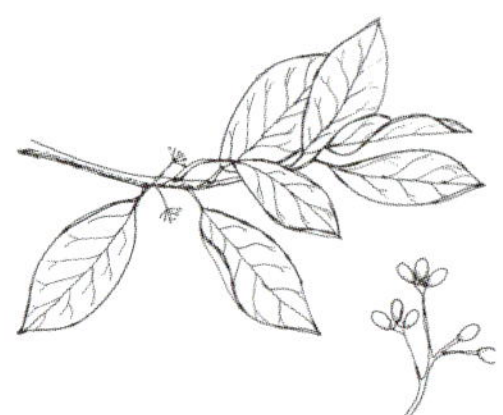

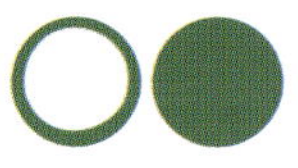

sun

soils

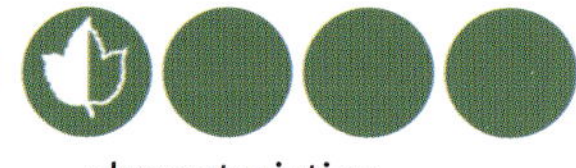

characteristics

- Leaves turn red in early fall
- Branches out at right angles
- Great pollinator
- More adaptive than Water Tupelo

plant communities

[1a 1b 1c] [2a 2b 2c] [3a 3b] [4a 4b] [5a 5b 5c]

Populus deltoides

Cottonwood

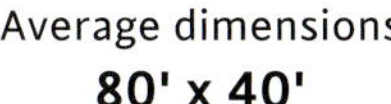

- Tall tree
- Straight trunk
- Open form
- Large leaves that delicately move with the wind
- Fast-growing tree
- Leaves are large and thick and carpet the ground for well over a month in fall; they do not decompose quickly
- Seed pods open to reveal seeds that resemble cotton balls, which can be messy in late summer

plant communities

[1a 1b 1c] [2a 2b 2c] [3a 3b] [4a 4b] [5a 5b 5c]

Quercus alba

White Oak

Average dimensions
60–100' x 50'

sun soils characteristics

- Large shade tree
- High canopy is common
- Vibrant red fall color
- Great pollinator
- Provides fruits and seeds
- Good nesting for birds

plant communities
[1a **1b 1c**] [2a 2b 2c] [3a 3b] [4a 4b] [5a 5b 5c]

Quercus lyrata

Overcup Oak

Average dimensions
80' x 100'

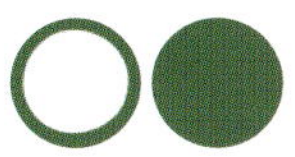

sun soils characteristics

- Great pollinator
- Very large trees when mature

plant communities

[1a 1b 1c] [2a 2b 2c] [3a 3b] [4a 4b] [5a 5b 5c]

Quercus michauxii

Cow Oak

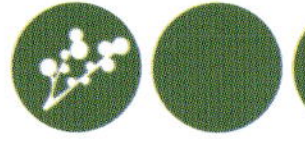

sun soils characteristics

Average dimensions
100' x 60'

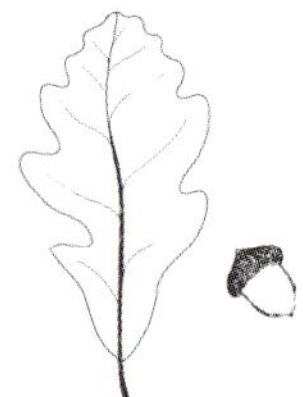

- Large shade tree with dense canopy
- Large leaves
- Messy in fall, but leaves beautiful red fall color
- Great pollinator

plant communities

[1a 1b 1c] [2a 2b 2c] [3a 3b] [4a 4b] [5a 5b 5c]

Quercus nigra

Water Oak

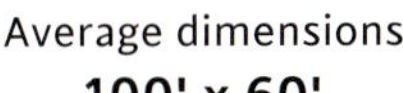
Average dimensions
100' x 60'

sun

soils

characteristics

- Large, semi-evergreen shade tree
- Weak-wooded and poor wind resistance
- Not recommended near structures
- Messy, frequently dropping branches
- Provides habitat for birds, squirrels, and wildlife

plant communities
[1a 1b 1c] [2a 2b 2c] [3a 3b] [4a 4b] [5a 5b 5c]

Quercus nuttallii

Nuttall Oak

Average dimensions
100' x 40'

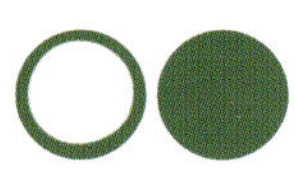

sun

soils

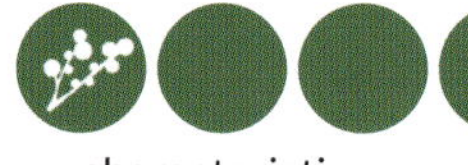

characteristics

- Large shade tree with open form
- Irregular branching
- Great for parking lots and gathering areas

plant communities

[1a 1b 1c] [2a 2b 2c] [3a 3b] [4a 4b] [5a 5b 5c]

Quercus phellos

Willow Oak

Average dimensions
50' x 70'

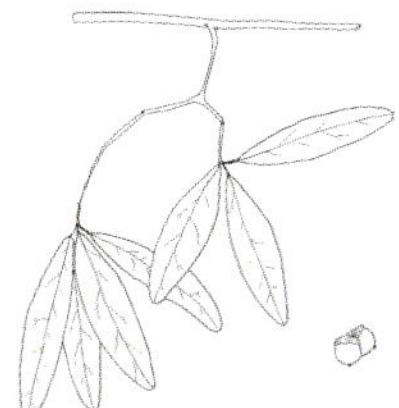

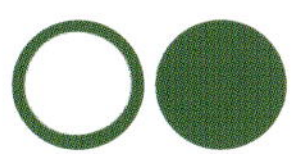
sun

soils

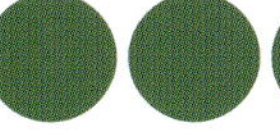
characteristics

- Large shade tree with dense canopy
- Good for shading paved areas like parking lots in association with BMPs
- Non-aggressive root systems, but like all oaks, should not be planted near structures
- Great pollinator

plant communities

[1a 1b 1c] [2a 2b 2c] [3a 3b] [4a 4b] [5a 5b 5c]

Salix nigra

Black Willow

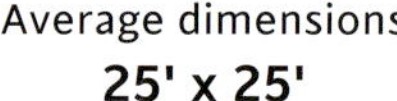

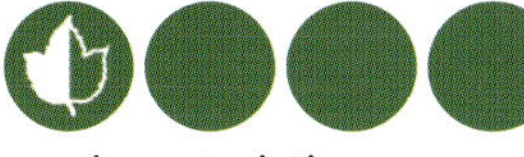

- Fast-growing upright tree
- Weak-wooded
- Usually a sign of the presence of water
- Early successional species in wet areas
- Can be planted in tight clumps for shore stabilization
- Usually not the best for wetlands or ponds
- Tends to attract mosquitoes

plant communities

[1a 1b 1c] [2a 2b 2c] [3a 3b] [4a 4b] [5a 5b 5c]

Taxodium ascendens

Pond Cypress

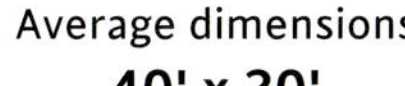

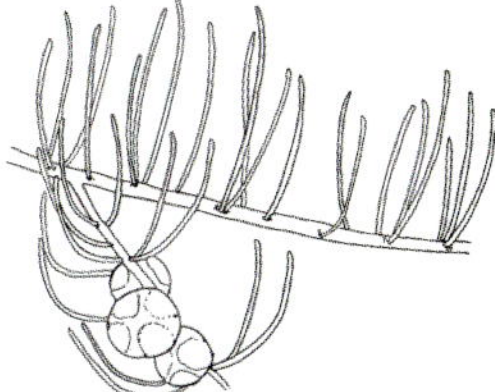

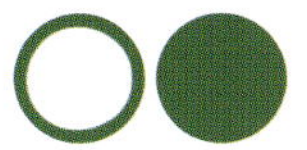

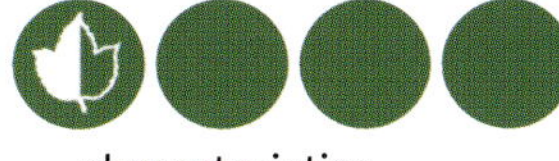

sun soils characteristics

- Very similar to Bald Cypress, but less propensity to make knees
- Upright form
- Vibrant bronze fall color
- Leaves spiral around branch, usually standing completely upright

plant communities

[1a 1b **1c**] [2a 2b 2c] [**3a** 3b] [4a 4b] [5a 5b 5c]

Taxodium distichum

Bald Cypress

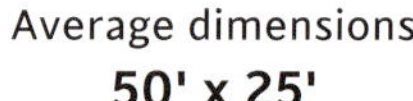

- Long-lived
- Upright form
- Regular, dense branching when young
- Irregular, open branching with age
- Grows well in wet or dry soils; more prone to knees in wet soil
- Can be planted densely for screening
- Good wind barriers
- Good for bosque-type seating areas
- Vibrant bronze fall color

plant communities

[1a 1b 1c] [2a 2b 2c] [3a 3b] [4a 4b] [5a 5b 5c]

Ulmus americana

American Elm

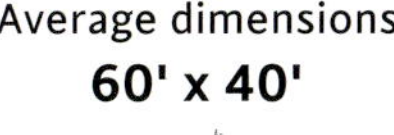

Average dimensions
60' x 40'

sun soils characteristics

- Large vase shape form with a high canopy
- Medium-dense branching
- Relatively fast growing when young
- Can become weak with advanced age
- Great patio and parking lot shade tree
- Provides fruits and seeds
- Good nesting for birds
- Vibrant yellow fall color

plant communities

[1a 1b 1c] [2a 2b 2c] [3a 3b] [4a 4b] [5a 5b 5c]

Evergreen Trees
for Stormwater Management

Evergreen Trees Master List

for Stormwater Management

Ilex opaca

American Holly

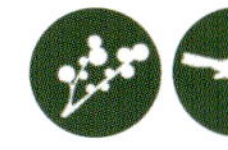

sun soils characteristics

Average dimensions
40' x 30'

- Dense holly with conical form
- Beautiful red berries in winter
- Good evergreen screen
- Good wind barriers
- Provides fruits and seeds
- Good nesting for birds

plant communities
[1a 1b **1c**] [2a 2b 2c] [3a 3b] [4a 4b] [5a 5b 5c]

Ilex vomitoria

Yaupon

Average dimensions
25' x 15'

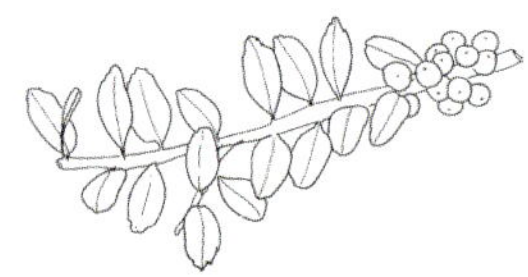

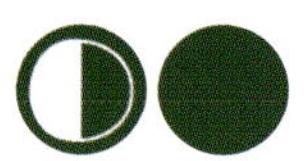

sun soils characteristics

- Large shrub or small tree
- Grows in dense thickets
- Great for small-scale screening
- Provides fruits and seeds
- Good nesting for birds
- Irregular form
- Fruit is mildly toxic

plant communities

[1a 1b 1c] [2a 2b 2c] [3a 3b] [4a 4b] [5a 5b 5c]

Magnolia virginiana

Sweet Bay Magnolia

Average dimensions
60' x 40'

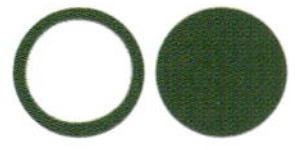

sun soils characteristics

- Slow growing
- Upright form
- Leaves have soft, silvery underside
- Small fragrant white flowers in spring
- Small to medium tree, but given the right conditions it can get rather large
- Highly adaptive to a wide range of conditions

plant communities

[1a **1b 1c**] [2a 2b 2c] [3a 3b] [4a 4b] [5a 5b 5c]

Myrica cerifera

Southern Wax Myrtle

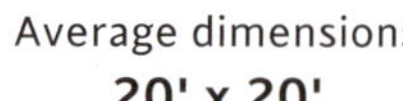

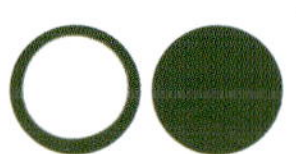

- Fast growing
- Large shrub or small tree
- Occurs naturally near water's edge
- Pungent flowers in early spring
- Good tree for screening
- Pedestrian-scale small tree
- Provides fruits and seeds
- Good nesting for birds
- Relatively short-lived
- Leaves produce oils that act as natural insect repellent

plant communities

[1a 1b 1c] [2a 2b 2c] [3a 3b] [4a 4b] [5a 5b 5c]

Quercus virginiana

Southern Live Oak

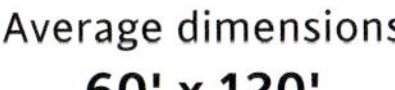

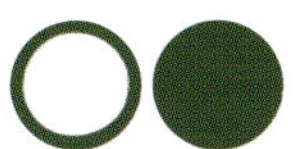

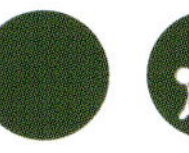
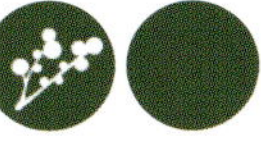

sun soils characteristics

- Large evergreen canopy tree
- Graceful, arching branches
- Very sensitive root system; water should not puddle at the base of this tree
- Great pollinator
- During construction, adding fill or cutting grade below the tree's drip zone can cause serious damage
- Butterfly larval food source
- Signature southern tree

plant communities

[1a 1b 1c] [2a 2b 2c] [3a 3b] [4a 4b] [5a 5b **5c**]

Deciduous Shrubs

for Stormwater Management

Deciduous Shrubs Master List
for Stormwater Management

Aesculus pavia

Red Buckeye

Average dimensions
20' x 10'

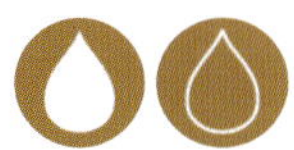

sun soils characteristics

- Large shrub to small tree; open form
- Reddish-fuschia flower spikes
- Fruit is poisonous to humans and livestock
- Good nectar source for hummingbirds and butterflies

plant communities

[1a 1b **1c**] [2a 2b 2c] [3a 3b] [4a 4b] [5a 5b 5c]

Baccharis halimifolia

Groundsel Bush

Average dimensions
8' x 6'

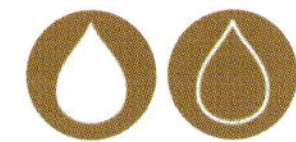
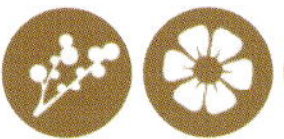

sun soils characteristics

- Provides fruits and seeds
- Good nesting for birds
- Leaves are poisonous to livestock
- Grows in irregularly flooded tidal fresh and brackish marshes, back dunes and inland open woods, vacant fields, and desert habitats

plant communities

[1a 1b 1c] [2a **2b** 2c] [3a 3b] [4a 4b] [**5a** 5b 5c]

Callicarpa americana

American Beautyberry

Average dimensions
6' x 6'

sun soils characteristics

- Round form
- Bright purple berries in fall, fading in winter
- Provides fruit and seeds
- Good nesting for birds

plant communities

[1a 1b **1c**] [2a **2b** 2c] [3a 3b] [4a 4b] [5a 5b 5c]

Cephalanthus occidentalis

Button Bush

Average dimensions
20' x 10'

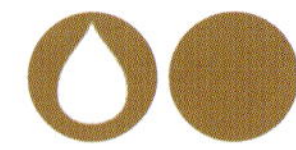

sun soils characteristics

- Open form with medium-texture leaves
- Attractive flowers in spring
- Great pollinator
- Good nectar source for butterflies
- Attractive flower balls

plant communities

[1a 1b 1c] [2a 2b 2c] [3a 3b] [4a 4b] [5a 5b 5c]

Hibiscus coccineus

Native Red Hibiscus

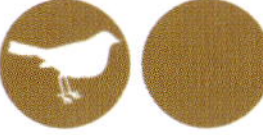

sun soils characteristics

Average dimensions
6' x 4'

- Medium-sized shrub, bright green foliage
- Flowers in spring, summer, and into fall
- Good nectar source for butterflies and hummingbirds
- Easily seeded and propogated

plant communities

[1a 1b 1c] [2a 2b 2c] [3a 3b] [4a 4b] [5a 5b 5c]

Hibiscus militaris

Solider Mallow

Average dimensions
6' x 5'

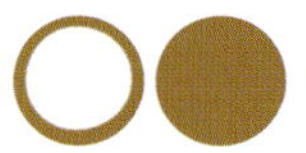

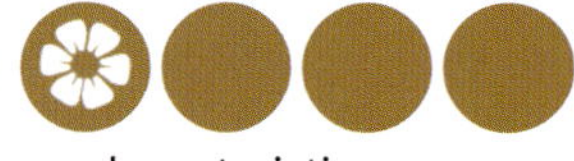

sun soils characteristics

- Large shrub in wetland areas
- Irregular, open form
- Not readily available in the trade but propagated by seeds and cuttings
- Colonizer

plant communities

[1a 1b 1c] [2a 2b 2c] [3a 3b] [4a 4b] [5a 5b 5c]

Hydrangea quercifolia

Oakleaf Hydrangea

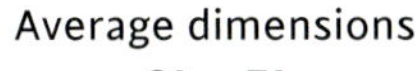

Average dimensions
8' x 5'

sun

soils

characteristics

- Large shrub with showy white flowers
- Very irregular form; can be spindly
- Available in both dwarf and regular varieties
- “Pee Wee” and “Sikes Dwarf” are common dwarf varieties

plant communities

[1a **1b** 1c] [2a 2b 2c] [3a 3b] [4a 4b] [5a 5b 5c]

Itea virginica

Virginia Willow

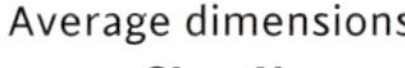

sun soils characteristics

- Small shrub
- Arching form with light green, soft leaves
- White flowers in spring are somewhat showy
- Fall color in cultivars such as "Henry's Garnet" can be very showy
- Medium-rate spreading shrub

plant communities

[1a 1b 1c] [2a 2b 2c] [3a 3b] [4a 4b] [5a 5b 5c]

Rhododendron canescens

Honeysuckle Azalea

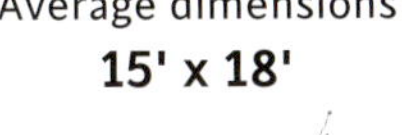

sun soils characteristics

- Small, open-form shrub
- Showy flowers in early spring
- Good nectar source for hummingbirds

plant communities

[1a **1b** 1c] [2a 2b 2c] [3a 3b] [4a 4b] [5a 5b 5c]

Sambucus canadensis

Elderberry

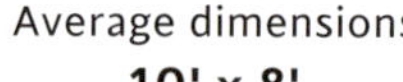

10' x 8'

sun soils characteristics

- Provides fruits and seeds
- Good nesting for birds
- Semi-woody plant structure

plant communities

[1a 1b 1c] [2a 2b 2c] [3a 3b] [4a 4b] [5a 5b 5c]

Viburnum dentatum

Arrowwood

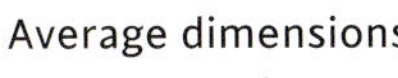

Average dimensions
15' x 6'

sun

soils

characteristics

- Dense, arching form
- Great pollinator; provides fruits, seeds, and good nesting for birds
- Good nectar source for butterflies
- Small white flowers in spring

plant communities

[1a **1b** 1c] [2a 2b 2c] [3a 3b] [4a 4b] [5a 5b **5c**]

Evergreen Shrubs
for Stormwater Management

full sun
filtered sun
partial sun
wet soils
moist soils
dry soils
fruiting bodies
seasonal color
flowering
attracts wildlife

Evergreen Shrubs Master List

for Stormwater Management

Ilex glabra

Inkberry

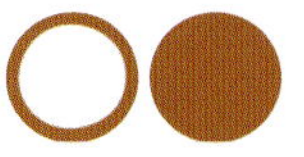

sun soils characteristics

Average dimensions
8' x 5'

- Salt tolerant
- Great pollinator
- Provides fruits, seeds, and good nesting for birds
- Dark green, waxy leaves

plant communities
[1a 1b 1c] [**2a** 2b 2c] [3a 3b] [4a 4b] [5a 5b 5c]

Illicium floridanum

Starbush

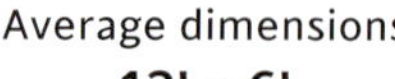

Average dimensions
12' x 6'

sun

soils

characteristics

- Bright burgundy flowers in spring
- Large, dense shrub
- Flowers used as spice in cooking

plant communities

[1a **1b** 1c] [2a 2b 2c] [3a 3b] [4a 4b] [5a 5b 5c]

Illicium parviflorum

Anise, Ocala Anise

Average dimensions
12' x 10'

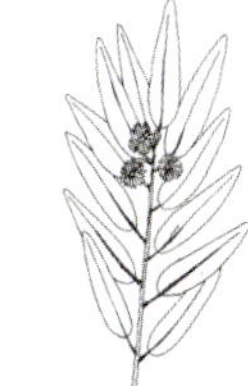

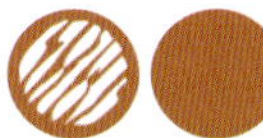

sun soils characteristics

- Small yellow flowers in spring
- Large, dense shrub
- Loose and wild form if not trimmed

plant communities

[1a 1b 1c] [2a **2b** 2c] [3a 3b] [4a 4b] [5a 5b 5c]

Leucothoe axillaris

Dog Hobble

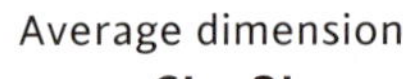

sun soils characteristics

- Tough evergreen foliage
- Dense plant with arching branches
- Concealed drooping white flowers

plant communities

[1a **1b** 1c] [2a 2b 2c] [3a 3b] [4a 4b] [5a 5b 5c]

Lyonia lucida

Fetterbush

Average dimensions
5' x 5'

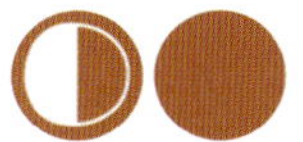

sun soils characteristics

- Very shade tolerant, but can take sun
- Dark green, waxy leaves
- Good source of nectar for butterflies
- Great pollinator

plant communities
[1a **1b 1c**] [2a 2b 2c] [3a 3b] [4a 4b] [5a 5b 5c]

Sabal minor

Dwarf Palmetto

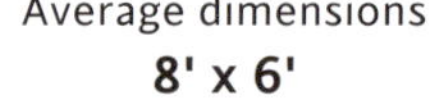

Average dimensions
8' x 6'

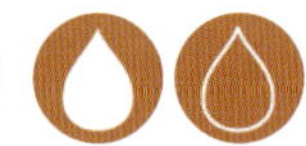

sun soils characteristics

- Dense cluster of fronds radiating out from center of the plant
- Slow growers; can develop trunk with extreme age
- Provides fruits and seeds
- Good nesting for birds
- Good pollinator

plant communities
[1a 1b **1c**] [**2a 2b** 2c] [3a 3b] [4a 4b] [5a 5b **5c**]

Grasses and Ferns

for Stormwater Management

Grasses and Ferns Master List

for Stormwater Management

Chasmanthium latifolium

Sea Oats

Average dimensions
2'–4'

sun

soils

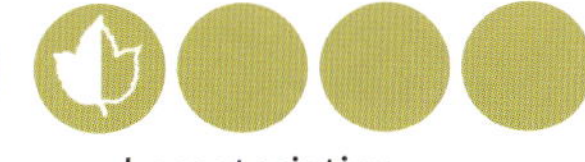
characteristics

- Soft-textured grass
- Pronounced seed pods are showy in the summer and fall, and move in the wind
- Small- to medium-sized grass plant
- Good for mass-planting on low slopes

plant communities

[1a **1b** 1c] [2a 2b 2c] [3a 3b] [4a 4b] [5a **5b** 5c]

Cyperus odoratus

Flatsedge

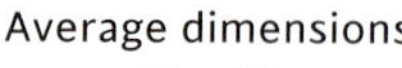

sun soils characteristics

- Emersed plants
- Occur in or near water's edge
- Puffy green flower spikes in summer
- Considered invasive in Florida

plant communities

[1a 1b 1c] [2a 2b 2c] [3a 3b] [4a 4b] [5a 5b 5c]

Juncus effusus

Soft Rush

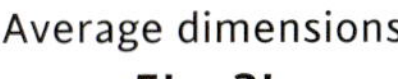

Average dimensions

5' x 3'

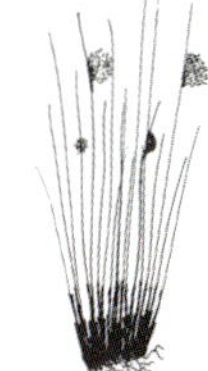

sun

soils

characteristics

- Naturally occurs along water's edge
- One of the first to establish in newly built ponds and wetlands
- Some varieties have showy inflorescence
- Provides fruits and seeds
- Good nesting for birds

plant communities

[1a 1b 1c**]** [2a 2b 2c] [3a 3b] [4a 4b] [5a 5b 5c]

Muhlenbergia capillaris

Gulf Muhly

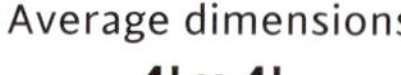
Average dimensions
4' x 4'

sun

soils

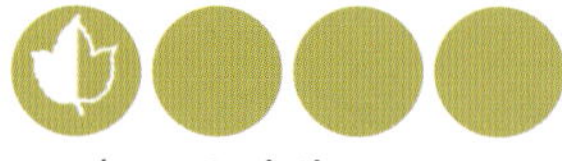
characteristics

- Small- to medium-sized perennial grass
- Inflorescence develops in late spring and remains throughout winter
- Attractive pink color in fall
- Dozens of varieties
- Varies in size and color depending on variety

plant communities

[1a 1b **1c**] [2a 2b 2c] [3a 3b] [4a 4b] [5a 5b 5c]

Onoclea sensibilis

Sensitive Fern, Bead Fern

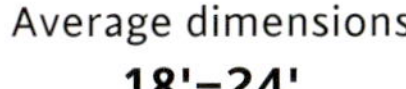

Average dimensions
18'–24'

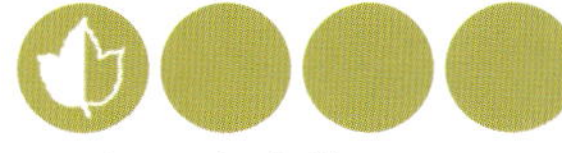

sun soils characteristics

- Relatively large fern
- Coarse-textured plant

plant communities
[1a 1b 1c] **[2a** 2b 2c**]** [3a 3b] [4a 4b] [5a 5b 5c]

Osmunda cinnamomea

Cinnamon Fern

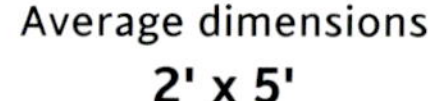

Average dimensions
2' x 5'

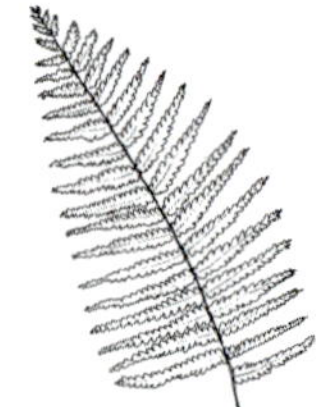

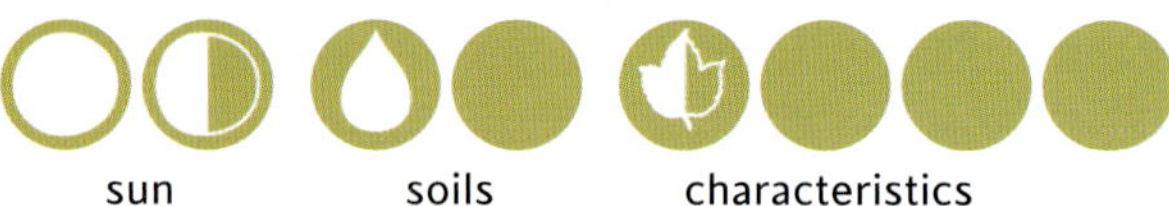

sun soils characteristics

- Occurs in understory colonies
- Light green foliage
- Showy swordlike floral spikes

plant communities

[1a 1b 1c] [**2a** 2b 2c] [3a 3b] [4a 4b] [5a 5b 5c]

Osmunda regalis

Royal Fern

Average dimensions

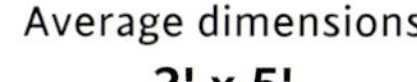

2' x 5'

- Adaptable
- Forms dense fern clumps
- Showy loose floral spikes

plant communities

[1a 1b 1c] [**2a** 2b 2c] [**3a** 3b] [4a 4b] [5a 5b 5c]

Scirpus acutus

Bulrush

Average dimensions
3' x 1'

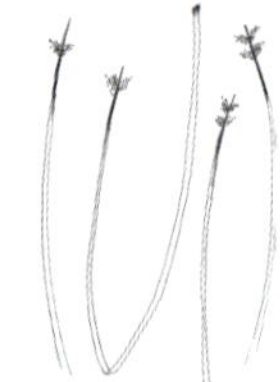

sun

soils

characteristics

- Large spiked grass
- Aggressive grower
- Good for shore stabilization

plant communities
[1a 1b 1c**]** [2a 2b 2c] [3a 3b] [4a 4b] [5a 5b 5c]

Scirpus cernuus

Fiber Optic Grass

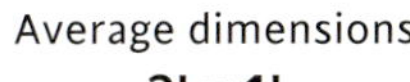

Average dimensions
2' x 1'

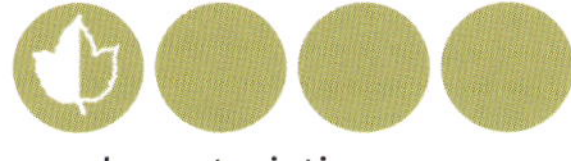

sun soils characteristics

- Showy small clumps
- Attractive flowers on leaf spikes

plant communities

[1a 1b 1c**]** [2a 2b 2c] **[3a** 3b**]** [4a 4b] [5a 5b 5c]

Thelypteris kunthii

Wood Fern

Average dimensions
3' x 3'

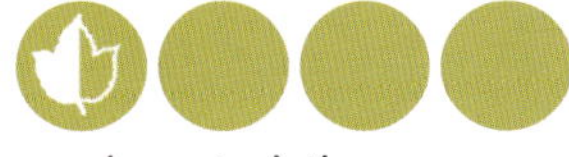

sun soils characteristics

- Perennial fern with large, light green leaves
- Usually in wet, shaded areas
- Adds a lower level texture to wooded areas

plant communities

[1a 1b **1c**] [**2a** 2b 2c] [3a 3b] [4a 4b] [5a 5b 5c]

Woodwardia virginica

Virginia Chain Fern

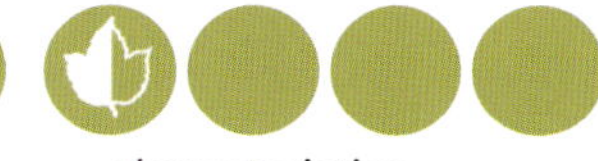

sun soils characteristics

Average dimensions
2' x 4'

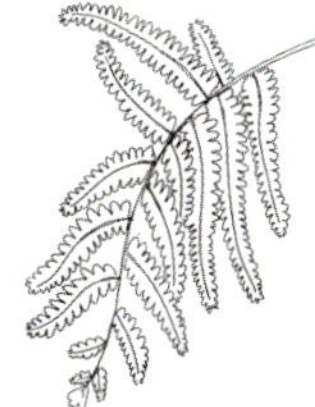

- Open-form clumps
- Bright yellow fall foliage
- Prominent brown spores on undersides

plant communities

[1a 1b 1c] [2a 2b 2c] [3a 3b] [4a 4b] [5a 5b 5c]

Perennials
for Stormwater Management

Perennials Master List
for Stormwater Management

Asclepias tuberosa

Butterfly Milkweed

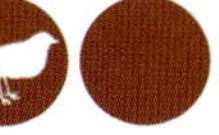

sun soils characteristics

- Great pollinator
- Butterfly larva food source
- Open, upright form
- Vibrant flower clumps at tops of stems

plant communities

[1a **1b** 1c] [2a 2b 2c] [3a 3b] [**4a** 4b] [5a 5b 5c]

Crinum species

Crinum Lily

sun soils characteristics

Average dimensions
1'–3'

- Dark green, straplike leaves
- Usually found in bayous, ditches, or other continually wet places
- Striking white flowers in early spring

plant communities

[1a 1b 1c] [2a 2b 2c] **[3a** 3b**]** [4a 4b] [5a 5b 5c]

Eupatorium coelestinum

Ageratum, Mist Flower

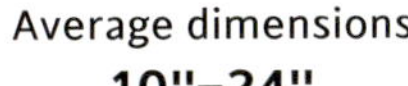

Average dimensions
10"–24"

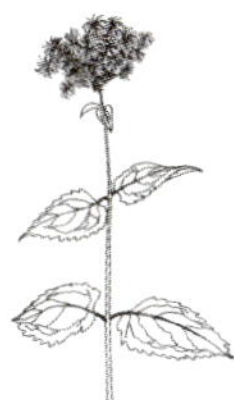

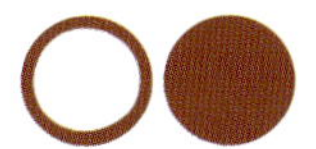

sun soils characteristics

- Flower is most appreciated when planted in clusters
- Open, leggy plant form

plant communities

[1a 1b 1c] [2a 2b 2c] [3a 3b] [**4a** 4b] [5a 5b **5c**]

Hymenocallis liriosme

Spider Lily, Swamp Lily

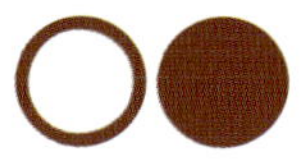

sun soils characteristics

Average dimensions
2' x 2'

- Dark green, straplike leaves
- Usually found in bayous, ditches, or other continually wet places
- Striking white flowers in early spring
- Shade tolerant

plant communities

[1a 1b 1c] [2a 2b 2c] [3a 3b] [4a 4b] [5a 5b 5c]

Iris louisiana

Louisiana Iris

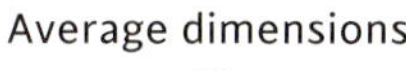

Average dimensions

2'

sun soils characteristics

- Simple strap-leaf plants
- Usually found in and around water
- Blooms in early spring
- Flower colors include reds, blues, yellows, and whites

plant communities

[1a 1b 1c] [2a 2b 2c] [3a 3b] [4a 4b] [5a 5b 5c]

Iris pseudacorus

Yellow Flag Iris

sun soils characteristics

Average dimensions

5'

- Hardy semi-evergreen Iris
- Naturalized to North America
- Aggressive clumping iris; could become invasive if left unmaintained

plant communities

[1a 1b 1c] [2a 2b 2c] [3a 3b] [4a 4b] [5a 5b 5c]

Lobelia cardinalis

Cardinal Flower

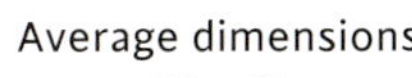

Average dimensions
2'– 4'

sun soils characteristics

- Disappearing from native habitat
- Good source of nectar for butterflies and hummingbirds
- Delicate, vibrant red flower spikes

plant communities

[1a **1b 1c**] [2a 2b 2c] [3a 3b] [4a 4b] [5a 5b 5c]

Ludwigia alternifolia

Bushy Seedbox

Average dimensions
2' x 3'

sun soils characteristics

- Does well on water's edge
- Soft, yellow flowers in spring and summer
- Low-growing, open form

plant communities

[1a 1b 1c] [2a 2b 2c] [3a 3b] **[4a** 4b**]** [5a 5b 5c]

Phytolacca americana

Pokeberry

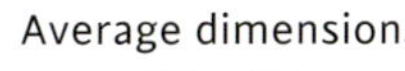

8' x 6'

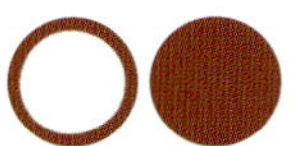

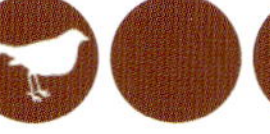

sun soils characteristics

- Borderline invasive in large areas of ideal growing conditions; use with caution
- Prominent flower and seed spikes
- Toxic to humans and livestock

plant communities

[1a 1b 1c] [2a 2b 2c] [3a 3b] [4a 4b] [5a 5b 5c]

Pontederia cordata

Pickerel Weed

Average dimensions
3' x 2'

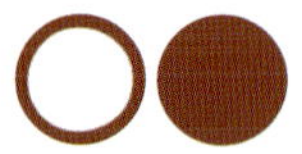

sun soils characteristics

- Colonizer in wet areas; can be invasive
- Good source of nectar for butterflies
- Showy purple flower spikes
- Grows well in understory, shaded conditions, and full sun

plant communities
[1a 1b 1c] [2a 2b 2c] **[3a 3b]** [4a **4b]** [5a 5b 5c]

Rudbeckia maxima

Coneflower

Average dimensions
5'– 6'

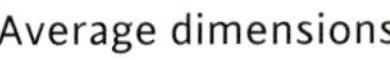

sun

soils

characteristics

- Profusely flowering perennial
- Low-mounding form
- Good for high-impact, sunny areas along with grasses

plant communities
[1a 1b 1c] [2a 2b 2c] [3a 3b] **[4a** 4b**]** [5a 5b 5c]

Sagittaria lancifolia

Bull Tongue Arrowhead

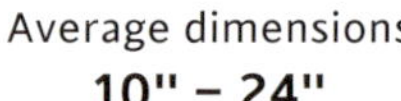

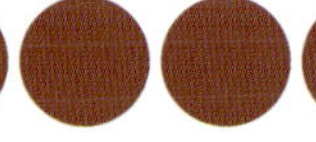

sun soils characteristics

- Colonizer in and along water
- White flowers

plant communities

[1a 1b 1c] [2a 2b 2c] [3a 3b] [4a **4b**] [5a 5b 5c]

Sarracenia species

Pitcher Plant

Average dimensions
2'

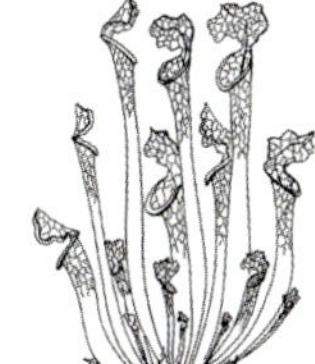

sun

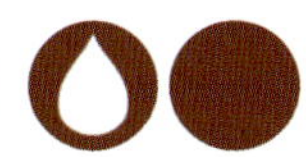

soils

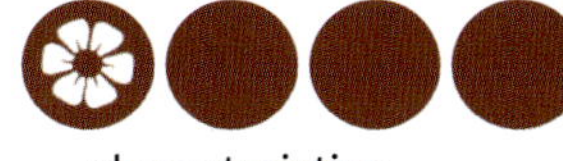

characteristics

- Bog conditions are ideal
- Grows specific to soil types
- Sculptural form
- Attractive flowers and stems vary in color

plant communities

[1a 1b 1c] [2a 2b 2c] [3a 3b] [4a 4b] [5a 5b 5c]

Saururus cernuus

Lizard's Tail

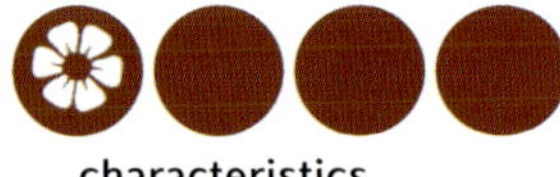

sun soils characteristics

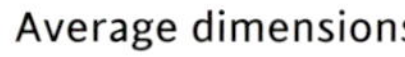
Average dimensions
1' – 3'

- Colonizes in wet and seasonably wet areas
- Best suited for large areas
- Arched white flowers

plant communities

[1a 1b 1c] [2a 2b 2c] [3a 3b] [4a 4b] [5a 5b 5c]

Solidago altissima

Goldenrod

Average dimensions
2' – 3'

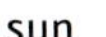

sun   soils   characteristics

- Good nectar source for butterflies
- Great pollinator
- Not responsible for pollen allergies associated with hay fever
- Occurs in colonies with grasses
- Early successional species

plant communities

[1a 1b 1c] [2a 2b 2c] [3a 3b] [**4a** 4b] [5a 5b 5c]

References

Online

"Online Plant Guide Search," OnlinePlantGuide.com, accessed September 13, 2012, http://www.onlineplantguide.com/.

"Tracking List and Fact Sheets," Louisiana Department of Wildlife and Fisheries, accessed September 13, 2012, http://www.wlf.louisiana. gov/wildlife/natural-communities-fact-sheets.

Print

Allen, Charles M., PhD, Dawn A. Newman, MS, and Harry H. Winters, MD *Grasses of Louisiana.* 3rd ed. Pitkin, LA: Allen's Native Ventures, LLC, 2004.

Allen, Charles M., PhD, Dawn A. Newman, MS, and Harry H. Winters, MD *Trees, Shrubs, and Woody Vines of Louisiana.* Pitkin, LA: Allen's Native Ventures LLC, 2002.

Brown, Clair A. *Louisiana Trees and Shrubs.* Baton Rouge: Claitor's Division, 1996.

Odenwald, Neil G., and James R. Turner. *Identification, Selection, and Use of Southern Plants for Landscape Design.* 4th ed. Baton Rouge: Claitor's Division, 2006.

Index

Botanical Name First

Index

Common Name First

About the Author

During her thirty-three years of experience as a landscape architect and planner, **Dana Nunez Brown** has worked for firms in New Orleans, Baton Rouge, Boston, and Orange County, California. She worked for EDAW Inc. and Parsons Brinckerhoff Inc. in California for over fifteen years before returning to Louisiana and settling in New Orleans, where she now serves as principal of Dana Brown & Associates Inc. Brown's work in Louisiana has focused on community planning, ecological design, and public outreach along with leading various Louisiana projects.

Brown worked tirelessly for two years to address the EPA and Louisiana Department of Environment Quality requirements for improving water quality in East Baton Rouge Parish. She not only helped revise chapters of the Unified Development Code, she also authored a manual to guide developers and other design professionals in the creation and implementation of stormwater best management practices. She periodically provides her expertise on low impact development, stormwater management, smart growth, and ecologically based development by making presentations at councils, universities, associations, and seminars across the state. She holds a BLA degree from Louisiana State University and an MLA degree from the Harvard Graduate School of Design and is a registered landscape architect licensed in the states of Louisiana, Mississippi, and California. Brown is also a LEED accredited professional, certified planner, and a member of the American Society of Landscape Architects (ASLA).